indulge it

indulge it

New Ideas for Delicious Desserts

RUNNING PRESS
PHILADELPHIA · LONDON

A QUINTET BOOK

© 1999 by Quintet Publishing Limited

First published in the United States of America in 1999
by Running Press Book Publishers

All rights reserved under the Pan-American and International
Copyright Conventions.

Printed in China by Leefung Asco Printers Ltd.

9 8 7 6 5 4 3 2 1

Digit on the right indicates the number of this printing

ISBN 0-7624-0501-5

Library of Congress
Cataloging-in-Publication Number 98-67647

This book was designed and produced by
Quintet Publishing Limited
6 Blundell Street
London N7 9BH

Creative Director: Rebecca Martin
Design: Deep Creative, London
Project Editor: Debbie Foy
Editor: Deborah Gray

Typeset in Great Britain by
Central Southern Typesetters, Eastbourne

This book may be ordered by mail from the publisher.
Please include $2.50 for postage and handling.
But try your bookstore first!

Running Press Book Publishers
125 South Twenty-second Street
Philadelphia, Pennsylvania 19103-4399

Because of the slight risk of salmonella, raw
eggs should not be served to the very young,
the ill or the elderly, or to pregnant women.

contents

introduction

A dessert should be decadent and **indulge it** will not disappoint. Packed with sumptuous sweets, **indulge it** provides the kind of desserts that will be the crowning glory to any meal, delicious drinks that satisfy every craving, and cookies and cakes that will make a wicked teatime treat.

All chocolate junkies should report here to languish in some serious dessert therapy. Get hooked on Chocolate Cookie Dough Ice Cream or Chocolate Soufflé, then feed your habit with Chocolate Banoffee Tart, Triple Chocolate Chunk Cookies, or Double Chocolate Chip Muffins.

For coffee-lovers, your ambrosia is fused with a host of recipes for your delectation and delight. Wake up with Creamy Iced Coffee or an Honest Coffee Shake, followed up by Coffee and Raisin Pecan Pie, Cappuccino Ice Cream, or a Coffee and Almond Pavlova.

Get hot and fruity with Cherry Jubilee flambé over an Extra-Rich Vanilla Ice Cream, Chocolate Coconut Cake or Orange Cardamom Tart. Shake it up with decadent drinks such as Double Fudge Treat, Hot Chocolate Float, and Marshmallow Foam, or rise to the challenge of mouth watering breads from around the globe. Try deep fried Rice Fritters, Czechoslovakian Christmas Bread, moist with fruit, nuts, and spices, or go for classic tea timers like Gingerbread or traditional English Scones.

Whatever your indulgence, **indulge it** can supply it—and more...

shake i

drinks

double fudge shake

Ingredients

SERVES 1

1 CUP WHOLE MILK

**3 SCOOPS FUDGE CHUNK
OR TOFFEE RIPPLE ICE CREAM**

1/4 CUP COLD FUDGE SAUCE

**1 TBSP ROASTED ALMONDS,
CHOPPED**

Place milk and 2 scoops of ice cream in a blender and process until just smooth. Avoid overblending, particularly if you are using textured fudge chunk ice cream, otherwise the chunks will be blended into the shake. Pour shake into a chilled glass and top with additional scoop of ice cream. Drizzle over fudge sauce and sprinkle with nuts.

Ingredients

SERVES 1

1/2 CUP WHOLE MILK

1 SCOOP RICH
CHOCOLATE ICE CREAM

1 SCOOP VANILLA ICE CREAM

1 TBSP BUTTERSCOTCH SAUCE

1 TBSP SEMISWEET
CHOCOLATE CHIPS

FOR THE TOPPING

1 SCOOP VANILLA ICE CREAM

BUTTERSCOTCH SAUCE

UNSALTED PEANUTS OR ALMONDS,
TOASTED AND CHOPPED

Blend together milk, chocolate, and vanilla ice cream, and butterscotch sauce. Pour into a glass, then stir in chocolate chips by hand. Top with more vanilla ice cream and drizzle over plenty of butterscotch sauce. Sprinkle with chopped nuts. You can go a step further and decorate the glass with a caramel star.

chocolate shake

Ingredients

SERVES 1

1 CUP WHOLE MILK

**1 SCOOP CHOCOLATE
ICE CREAM**

Place milk and ice cream in a blender
and process until smooth. Pour into a
chilled glass and serve.

Chocolate Shake Variations

Adult Chocolate Chip: As above,
but also add 2 tablespoons brandy,
Cointreau, crème de caçao, Amaretto,
or Irish Cream.

After Dinner Chocolate: Stir 2 to 3
crushed after dinner mints in by hand—
pick ones with crunchy mint pieces.

Chocolate Banana: Add 1 small banana
with chocolate ice cream and milk.

Neapolitan: Stir ¼ cup chopped
fresh strawberries into shake by
hand. Top with strawberry sauce and
toasted coconut.

hot chocolate float

Ingredients

SERVES 4

$^{1}/_{3}$ CUP SEMISWEET CHOCOLATE CHIPS

3 TBSP SUPERFINE SUGAR

$1^{1}/_{4}$ CUPS WATER

2 CUPS WHOLE MILK

$^{1}/_{4}$ CUP LIGHT CREAM

$^{1}/_{2}$ TSP VANILLA EXTRACT

4 SCOOPS VANILLA ICE CREAM

CHOCOLATE POWDER OR GROUND CINNAMON, TO DECORATE

Place chocolate chips, sugar, and water in a saucepan and bring to a boil, stirring constantly for 2 minutes. Stir in milk, cream, and vanilla and heat through—do not boil. Beat with a wire whisk until frothy, then pour into four warmed mugs.

Carefully place a scoop of ice cream into each mug and sprinkle with chocolate powder or cinnamon. Serve immediately.

creamy iced coffee

Ingredients

SERVES 2

1 CUP WHOLE MILK

1⅓ CUPS DOUBLE STRENGTH HOT COFFEE

CRUSHED ICE

COFFEE SYRUP, TO TASTE

3 TBSP HEAVY CREAM, LIGHTLY WHIPPED
UNTIL THICK AND SOFT

COFFEE SUGAR CRYSTALS, TO DECORATE

Heat milk until almost at a boil, then add to the coffee and stir. Leave to cool, then chill for 30 minutes to 1 hour.

Place 2 or 3 tablespoons of crushed ice in two tall glasses, then pour chilled coffee over. Adjust to taste with coffee syrup.

Top with the lightly whipped cream and a few sugar crystals for decoration. Serve immediately, with a long swizzle stick in each glass to stir up the coffee and ice.

Coffee Syrup

The amount of sugar added to a coffee shake is an individual matter. Even people who take their hot coffee without sugar will find that the flavor of a shake is improved with a little sugar or better still, coffee syrup. The sugar needs to be added to the blender and the syrup can be added afterwards, drop by drop, until it is just right.

Make coffee syrup by adding 6 scoops of coffee to 1 cup of boiling water. Infuse for 10 minutes, then strain. This will make about ³⁄₄ cup coffee. Add ³⁄₄ cup sugar and heat gently until dissolved. This syrup is too sweet to form the basis for a coffee shake but is the best sweetener.

Place in a sterilized bottle and it will keep for one month in the refrigerator.

honest coffee shake

Ingredients

SERVES 1

**1 CUP STRONG COFFEE
(INSTANT OR GROUND),
CHILLED**

**1/2 CUP WHOLE MILK
OR HALF-AND-HALF**

1 SCOOP COFFEE ICE CREAM

ICE

1/2-2 TSP COFFEE SYRUP
(SEE P.13)

FOR THE TOPPING

**WHIPPED HEAVY CREAM
(OPTIONAL)**

Place the coffee, milk or half-and-half, and ice cream in a blender along with ice, if your blender can take it. Process until smooth. Pour into a glass with a little more ice and sweeten to taste with coffee syrup. Top with whipped heavy cream, if desired.

coffee eggnog

Ingredients

SERVES 2

1 TSP SOFT BROWN SUGAR

1 EGG YOLK (SEE NOTE, P.4)

1 CUP WHOLE MILK

1 CUP STRONG HOT COFFEE

2 CINNAMON STICKS

Beat sugar and egg yolk with a small whisk until creamy. Heat milk until almost at a boil, then add to the egg with the hot coffee, whisking all the time. Pour into mugs, and stir coffee with cinnamon sticks, adding a little extra sugar if necessary.

mocha milk shake

Ingredients

SERVES 2

1 CUP COLD BLACK COFFEE

1 TBSP COFFEE ESSENCE

1 CUP WHOLE MILK

**2 SCOOPS CHOCOLATE
ICE CREAM**

1 BANANA, CHOPPED

1 CUP CRUSHED ICE

**CRUSHED FLAKED CHOCOLATE,
TO DECORATE**

Process all the ingredients together in a blender until thick and smooth, then pour into tall glasses. Alternatively, pour milk shake into two glasses filled with crushed ice.

Top with flaked or shredded chocolate and serve immediately.

marshmallow foam

Ingredients

SERVES 1

1 CUP WHOLE MILK

¹/₄ CUP MINI MARSHMALLOWS

2 SCOOPS RASPBERRY ICE CREAM

MINI MARSHMALLOWS OR 1 LARGE TOASTED MARSHMALLOW, TO DECORATE

Heat milk and marshmallows until the marshmallows are beginning to melt, then chill in the refrigerator. Place in a blender with raspberry ice cream and process until smooth and very foamy. Pour into a glass and serve decorated with a few mini marshmallows or 1 large toasted marshmallow on a toothpick.

key lime

Ingredients

SERVES 1

¹/₂ LEMON

¹/₂ LIME

1¹/₂-2 TBSP SUGAR

1 CUP WHOLE MILK

2 SCOOPS VANILLA ICE CREAM

3 TBSP SEMISWEET CHOCOLATE CHIPS OR SPRINKLES

WHIPPED HEAVY CREAM

SEMISWEET CHOCOLATE CHIPS OR SPRINKLES AND CITRUS PEEL CURLS, TO DECORATE

Wash lemon and lime well and cut into pieces. Place in blender with the sugar and milk and process until only tiny flecks of rind are visible. Sift through a non-metallic strainer, pressing out all the liquid.

Return to blender and add ice cream. Process until smooth. Pour and stir in chocolate chips or sprinkles. Top with whipped heavy cream and decorate with chocolate chips or sprinkles and citrus peel curls. For a smoother shake, simply omit the chocolate chips or sprinkles.

cool it

ice creams & sauces

chocolate cookie dough

Ingredients

SERVES 4

1¹/₄ CUPS LIGHT CREAM

1 VANILLA BEAN

4 EXTRA-LARGE EGG YOLKS

¹/₂ CUP SUGAR

1¹/₄ CUPS HEAVY CREAM

FOR THE COOKIE DOUGH

1 CUP FLOUR

1 TBSP UNSWEETENED
COCOA POWDER, SIFTED

5¹/₃ TBSP (²/₃ STICK)
UNSALTED BUTTER

¹/₃ CUP SUGAR

¹/₃ CUP CHOCOLATE
CHIPS, CHOPPED

WATER TO MIX, IF NECESSARY

Make up a quantity of Extra-Rich Vanilla Ice Cream following the method on page 30.

Prepare cookie dough while custard for the ice cream is cooling. Blend together flour, cocoa, and butter. Stir in sugar and chocolate chips, then bring the mixture together into firm dough, adding a few drops of water to mix if necessary. Knead dough thoroughly, then cover with plastic wrap and chill. (You will need about half the dough for the ice cream, but it is difficult to make a smaller quantity. Add more if you wish, or freeze remainder for later use.) Chop the dough roughly before you add it to the cream.

Freeze ice cream as instructed on page 30, then fold in as much chopped dough as your conscience will allow. Continue churning, or harden in the freezer before serving.

white chocolate chunk

Ingredients

SERVES 4

2¹/₂ CUPS MILK

¹/₄ CUP SUGAR

³/₄ CUP WHITE CHOCOLATE, CHOPPED ROUGHLY

1 TSP VANILLA EXTRACT

PINCH OF SALT

¹/₃ CUP WHITE CHOCOLATE CHIPS, CHOPPED ROUGHLY

¹/₄ CUP DARK CHOCOLATE CHIPS, CHOPPED ROUGHLY

Prepare basic ice milk following blueprint for Vanilla Ice Milk (see page 30), adding chopped white chocolate to the hot milk and stirring until it has melted. The finer you chop the chocolate, the quicker this will be; using a food processor is ideal. Leave mixture until completely cold.

Stir in vanilla and salt, then freeze the mixture as instructed. Add white and dark chocolate chips and continue churning until ready to serve.

mint chocolate chip

Ingredients

SERVES 4

1¹/₄ CUPS LIGHT CREAM

1 VANILLA BEAN

4 EXTRA-LARGE EGG YOLKS

¹/₂ CUP SUGAR

1¹/₄ CUPS HEAVY CREAM

3 TBSP CRÈME DE MENTHE

¹/₃ CUP CHOCOLATE CHIPS OR CHOCOLATE, CHOPPED ROUGHLY

Make up a batch of Extra-Rich Vanilla Ice Cream, following method on page 30, but add the crème de menthe to the custard just before cooling.

Freeze the ice cream as instructed until almost ready to serve, then add chocolate chips and finish churning.

cappuccino sherbert

Ingredients

SERVES 4

1/3 CUP COARSELY
GROUND COFFEE

2 1/2 CUPS HOT
(NOT BOILING) WATER

1/2 CUP SOFT BROWN
OR RAW CANE SUGAR

3/4 CUP HEAVY CREAM,
OR A BLEND OF HEAVY AND
LIGHT SHREDDED CHOCOLATE
AND SOFT BROWN SUGAR,
TO DECORATE

Mix coffee, water, and sugar together, stirring until sugar has dissolved. Leave until completely cold, then strain.

Stir the cream into strained coffee, then pour into an ice-cream machine and/or freeze-churn as for Extra-Rich Vanilla (page 30) until ready to serve.

Serve in cappuccino cups, sprinkled with shredded chocolate and sugar.

coffee ice cream & chocolate ripple

Ingredients

SERVES 6 TO 8

$^2/_3$ CUP HOT WATER

4 TBSP COARSELY GROUND HIGH ROAST COFFEE

4 EGG YOLKS

$^2/_3$ CUP SOFT BROWN SUGAR

$^1/_2$ TSP APPLE SPICE

1$^1/_4$ CUPS LIGHT CREAM

1$^1/_4$ CUPS HEAVY CREAM

FOR THE CHOCOLATE FUDGE SAUCE

3$^1/_2$ OZ SEMISWEET CHOCOLATE,
BROKEN INTO SMALL PIECES

3 TBSP LIGHT CORN SYRUP

2 TBSP HOT WATER

1 TSP COFFEE ESSENCE (OPTIONAL)

Pour hot water over the coffee and let stand for 10 minutes. Whisk egg yolks and sugar in a bowl with apple spice until pale and thick.

Strain coffee through a fine strainer into a pan with the light cream and heat gently until almost at a boil. Pour mixture onto the egg yolk mixture, stirring all the time. Rinse pan in cold water, return custard to the pan, and cook slowly until thickened just enough to coat the back of a wooden spoon. Transfer custard to a bowl. Let cool completely, then chill for 1 hour.

Meanwhile, make the sauce. Place all the ingredients in a heavy-bottomed pan and heat very gently until melted and blended together. Pour into a small bowl, allow to cool, then chill until required.

Fold heavy cream into chilled custard, then freeze the mixture as instructed for Extra-Rich Vanilla (page 30), until ready to serve.

Pack scoops of the ice cream into a clean freezer box, then spoon chocolate sauce over, pressing ice cream down so that there are no gaps. Harden for at least 30 minutes in freezer before serving.

cherry amaretto

Ingredients

SERVES 4

3 1/2 CUPS MILK

2/3 CUP SUGAR

**1 TSP VANILLA EXTRACT,
OR 2 TSP VANILLA ESSENCE**

PINCH OF SALT

**1/2 CUP CHERRIES, CHOPPED
ROUGHLY**

**1/4 CUP AMARETTI COOKIES,
CHOPPED ROUGHLY**

Prepare the basic ice milk following the blueprint recipe for Vanilla Ice Milk (see page 30).

Freeze cooled mixture as instructed until almost ready to serve. Fold in chopped cherries and cookies, then allow mixture to harden slightly in the freezer for 10 to 15 minutes before serving.

chocolate-orange sauce

Ingredients

SERVES 4

1¹/₃ CUPS BITTER CHOCOLATE
(USE CHIPS OR BROKEN INTO
SMALL SQUARES)

¹/₄ CUP LIGHT CORN SYRUP

1 TBSP (¹/₈ STICK)
UNSALTED BUTTER

²/₃ CUP LIGHT CREAM

1 ORANGE, SHREDDED
RIND AND JUICE

2-3 TBSP ORANGE LIQUEUR,
SUCH AS COINTREAU

This sauce may be made in a microwave or in a bowl over a pan of hot water. Heat chocolate, syrup, and butter together until melted, then stir in cream and whisk until thoroughly mixed. Add orange rind and juice, and the liqueur, then use as required.

cherry jubilee sauce

Ingredients

SERVES 4

1¹/₂ CUPS CANNED PITTED BLACK CHERRIES

2 LEVEL TSP ARROWROOT

1 CUP JUICE FROM THE CANNED CHERRIES

JUICE OF HALF A LEMON

¹/₄ CUP BRANDY

Drain cherries, reserving juice from the can, then cut fruits in half. Blend arrowroot with measured juice, then heat gently in a small saucepan until at a boil, when the sauce will clear. Stir in cherries with lemon juice, and cook for a further 1 minute, to heat the fruits.

Pour sauce into a warmed sauceboat or serving dish. Warm the brandy; the easiest way to do this is in a metal ladle over heat. Pour brandy over the sauce and light it immediately with a match.

Serve the cherry sauce over ice cream once flames have subsided.

butterscotch sauce

Ingredients

SERVES 4

3 TBSP (¹/₃ STICK) BUTTER

¹/₄ CUP SOFT BROWN SUGAR

2 TBSP LIGHT CORN SYRUP

¹/₂ CUP MILK

Heat butter, sugar, and syrup together in a small, heavy-bottomed pan until butter has melted and ingredients have blended together. Boil rapidly until mixture is at 235°F, soft ball stage (this should be marked on your sugar thermometer). Cool mixture slightly, then gradually beat in the milk. Use warm, or cool completely before serving.

extra-rich vanilla

Ingredients

SERVES 4

1¼ CUPS LIGHT CREAM
1 VANILLA BEAN
4 EXTRA-LARGE EGG YOLKS
½ CUP SUGAR
1¼ CUPS HEAVY CREAM

Heat light cream with the vanilla bean until almost at a boil, then remove pan from heat. Cover, leave for at least 20 minutes, or until cold, then remove vanilla bean. Whisk egg yolks and sugar together until thick and pale, but not too frothy.

Reheat cream until almost at a boil, then pour it onto the eggs, stirring all the time with a wooden spoon. Return custard to the rinsed pan and heat gently, stirring continuously, until the custard just coats the back of the spoon. Leave custard until cold, then chill thoroughly for at least 1 hour.

Lightly whip the heavy cream until thick and floppy, then fold it into chilled custard. Turn mixture into an ice-cream machine, and freeze-churn until ready to serve. Alternatively, place mixture in a freezer box and freeze for 45 minutes. Whip with a fork to break down ice crystals. Repeat freezing and whipping process at least twice more until ice cream is frozen and smooth, about 4 hours.

vanilla ice milk (blueprint recipe)

Ingredients

SERVES 4

3½ CUPS MILK
⅔ CUP SUGAR
1 TSP VANILLA EXTRACT
PINCH OF SALT

Heat milk until almost at a boil, when tiny bubbles are just rising to the surface. Add sugar and stir until dissolved, then leave milk to cool completely.

Stir vanilla and salt into the cold milk, then pour it into an ice-cream machine. Freeze-churn until thick and ready to serve or follow by-hand method for Extra-Rich Vanilla.

desire i

desserts & tarts

three-layered dessert

Ingredients

SERVES 4 TO 6

4 TBSP CORNSTARCH

4 CUPS WHOLE MILK

1 TSP VANILLA SUGAR

4 TBSP SUGAR

8 EGGS, SEPARATED
(SEE NOTE, P.4)

**SCANT 1 CUP READY-TO-EAT
PRUNES, PITTED**

2/3 CUP GRANULATED SUGAR

2 SMALL CINNAMON STICKS

1/3 CUP PORT

**SCANT 1 CUP
SUPERFINE SUGAR**

Dissolve cornstarch in 1/2 cup of the milk. Put remainder of milk in a saucepan, with vanilla sugar and the 4 tablespoons sugar, and warm over medium heat.

Whisk egg yolks, then add to saucepan, stirring. Continue to stir as you add the dissolved cornstarch. When mixture reaches a cream consistency, turn off heat.

In a saucepan, place prunes, granulated sugar, cinnamon sticks, port, and a generous 1/2 cup water. Bring to a boil, then cook until reduced, mashing prunes from time to time. When soft, turn off the heat. When both mixtures are cool, layer in a glass serving dish.

Beat egg whites until stiffly peaking. Then beat in superfine sugar. Using a large metal spoon, arrange the meringue on top of bowl in small peaks. Chill for 1 hour before serving.

brazilian coconut manjar

Ingredients

SERVES 4 TO 6

1 SACHET GELATIN

6 EGG WHITES (SEE NOTE, P.4)

14-OZ CAN SWEETENED CONDENSED MILK

1 CUP HEAVY CREAM

14-OZ CAN COCONUT MILK

1/2 CUP SHREDDED COCONUT, PREFERABLY FRESH

FOR THE SAUCE

3/4 CUP READY-TO-EAT PRUNES, PITTED

5 TBSP SUPERFINE SUGAR

Pour gelatin into 1/2 cup very hot water. Stir well to dissolve.

Beat the egg whites until softly peaking. Still beating, add condensed milk, cream, and coconut milk. Add dissolved gelatin, ensuring a smooth consistency. Then add shredded coconut. Pour mixture into a china bowl. Chill until needed.

For the sauce, in a small saucepan, put 3/4 cup water, the prunes, and the sugar. Bring to a boil, lower heat, and let simmer for a while. When you think that the prunes are a little softer, set aside a few whole prunes for decoration, then simmer the rest until soft. Set aside and let cool until just warm.

Serve the chilled manjar topped with warm prune sauce. Decorate with reserved whole prunes.

danish apple cake

Ingredients

SERVES 4 TO 6

3 CUPS FRESH WHOLE WHEAT BREAD CRUMBS

1/3 CUP RAW BROWN SUGAR

5 1/2 TBSP (2/3 STICK) UNSALTED BUTTER

1 LB PREPARED COOKING APPLES, PEELED, CORED, AND SLICED

SHREDDED RIND AND JUICE OF 1 LEMON

Mix bread crumbs with sugar. Melt butter in a large skillet, add crumb mixture, and fry quickly until the crumbs are crisp. Set aside until needed.

Cook apples with the lemon rind and juice and as little water as possible until soft. Allow to cool.

Turn half the apples into a glass dish, then make a layer of half the crumbs over the apples. Repeat layers, finishing with remaining crumbs. Let cool completely, then chill for at least 1 hour before serving.

banana custard

Ingredients

SERVES 3 TO 4

2 BANANAS, SLICED

SHREDDED RIND AND JUICE OF 1 LEMON

3 CUPS SOUR CREAM OR YOGURT

$^1/_2$ CUP PECANS, CHOPPED ROUGHLY

1 TBSP HONEY

$^1/_2$ CUP BRAN

WHOLE MILK

Toss banana slices in lemon juice, then place in a bowl. Carefully mix in sour cream or yogurt, nuts, honey, and bran. If mixture is very thick, add 1 or 2 tablespoons of milk to thin it down. Decorate with lemon rind just before serving.

coffee and almond pavlova

Ingredients

SERVES 8 TO 10

GENEROUS 1 CUP SUPERFINE
SUGAR, PLUS EXTRA FOR
SPRINKLING

$1/3$ CUP GROUND ALMONDS

1 TSP CREAM OF TARTAR

1 TBSP CORNSTARCH

4 EGG WHITES

PINCH OF SALT

$1/2$ TSP ALMOND EXTRACT

1 TSP WHITE WINE VINEGAR

2 TBSP COARSELY GROUND
HIGH ROAST COFFEE

5 TBSP HOT WATER

$1/4$ CUP BLANCHED ALMONDS

$1^{1}/4$ CUPS HEAVY CREAM

$1^{3}/4$ OZ SEMISWEET
CHOCOLATE, CHOPPED
ROUGHLY

Preheat a 300°F oven. Cover a cookie sheet with baking parchment and mark out a 10-inch circle. Scatter a little superfine sugar over the parchment.

Toast ground almonds under a medium broiler until golden, then let cool. Mix together sugar, cream of tartar, and cornstarch.

Whisk egg whites with salt until stiff. Add almond extract and whisk again. Gradually add sugar mixture. Whisk until just combined. Quickly fold in the vinegar and cold toasted almonds using a wire whisk.

Pile meringue onto cookie sheet, spreading it lightly over marked circle; fork up the edges into soft peaks. Bake for 2 hours. Turn off oven and leave meringue for 10 minutes more. Place on a wire rack to cool completely.

Meanwhile, pour hot water over the coffee and leave for 15 minutes. Strain, then let cool completely. Toast blanched almonds for 3 to 4 minutes under a medium broiler until browned. Cool and chop roughly.

Whip the cream until thick; then add cold coffee. Continue whipping until soft peaks form, then fold in chopped toasted almonds. Peel away paper from meringue base, and place on a large serving plate. Spoon coffee and almond cream onto meringue. Spread it over the center and fork it up gently into tiny peaks.

Melt chocolate in a bowl over a pan of hot water. Spoon melted chocolate into a wax paper piping bag, snip off the end, then drizzle chocolate over pavlova. Leave a few minutes before serving.

gingered crème brûlée tartlets

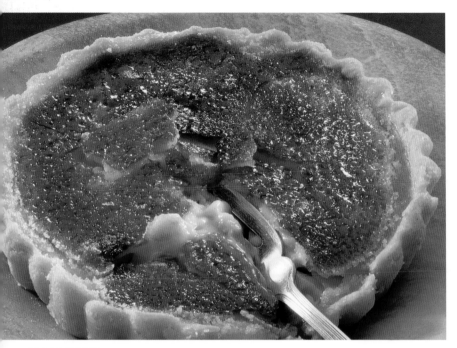

Ingredients

SERVES 4

FOUR 4-INCH TARTLET PANS LINED WITH BASIC SWEET PASTRY (SEE P.50)

1¼ CUPS HEAVY CREAM

1 EGG

2 EGG YOLKS

1 TBSP SUGAR

1 TBSP GINGER SYRUP (FROM THE BOTTLE)

1 PIECE BOTTLED PRESERVED GINGER, CHOPPED FINELY

¼–⅓ CUP GRANULATED BROWN SUGAR

Preheat a 325°F oven. Set tartlet cases on a cookie sheet.

In a small saucepan over medium heat, bring cream to a boil. Whisk egg and egg yolks with the sugar and ginger syrup until lightened, about 1 minute. Slowly whisk in the hot cream. Strain into a measuring cup and stir in chopped ginger.

Divide mixture evenly among tartlet cases. Bake until the custard is lightly set, about 15 minutes. Transfer to a wire rack to cool, then chill for at least 4 hours or overnight.

Just before serving, preheat broiler. Sprinkle a thin layer of granulated brown sugar evenly over custard, right to pastry edge. If pastry is already very brown, protect with a thin strip of foil while broiling. Broil close to the heat until sugar melts and begins to bubble, about 1 minute; do not overbroil or the custard will begin to curdle. Chill immediately to allow caramel to harden, about 5 minutes, then serve.

chocolate ganache
and berry tart

Ingredients

SERVES 6 TO 8

9-INCH TART PAN LINED
WITH CHOCOLATE PASTRY,
BAKED BLIND (SEE P.50)

2²/₃ CUPS HEAVY CREAM

1 CUP SEEDLESS
RASPBERRY PRESERVE

8 OZ GOOD QUALITY
SEMISWEET CHOCOLATE,
CHOPPED

¹/₄ CUP FRAMBOISE OR OTHER
RASPBERRY-FLAVORED LIQUEUR

1¹/₂ LB MIXED FRESH
SUMMER BERRIES, SUCH AS
RASPBERRIES, BLACKBERRIES,
STRAWBERRIES (QUARTERED
IF LARGE), LOGANBERRIES,
OR BLUEBERRIES

1-2 TBSP SUPERFINE SUGAR

In a saucepan over medium heat, bring 1²/₃ cups of cream and ³/₄ cup of raspberry preserve to a boil, whisking until it dissolves. Remove heat and add chocolate all at once, stirring until melted and smooth. Strain mixture directly into the pastry shell, lifting and turning the tart to distribute filling evenly. Cool completely or chill until set, at least 1 hour.

In a small saucepan over medium heat, heat remaining preserve and 2 tablespoons of the framboise or other raspberry-flavored liqueur until melted and bubbling. Drizzle over the berries and toss to coat well. Arrange berries over the top of the tart then chill until ready to serve.

Bring the tart to room temperature before serving. Whip the remaining cream with the sugar and remaining liqueur until soft peaks form. Spoon into a serving bowl and serve with tart.

chocolate soufflé tarts

Ingredients

SERVES 6 TO 8

**6-8 BRIOCHE MOLDS OR
OTHER DEEP TARTLET PANS
OR RAMEKINS, BUTTERED AND
LINED WITH CHOCOLATE PASTRY**
(SEE P.50)

**4 OZ SEMISWEET
CHOCOLATE, CHOPPED**

4 TBSP (½ STICK) BUTTER

4 EGGS, SEPARATED

2 TBSP BRANDY OR COGNAC

¼ TSP CREAM OF TARTAR

2 TBSP SUGAR

**CONFECTIONERS' SUGAR,
FOR DUSTING**

Preheat a 425°F oven. Set brioche molds, tartlet pans, or ramekins on a cookie sheet.

In a saucepan over low heat, melt chocolate and butter until smooth, stirring frequently. Remove from heat and beat in egg yolks, one at a time, then beat in the brandy. Set aside.

In a large bowl and with an electric mixer, beat egg whites and cream of tartar until softly peaking. Sprinkle in the sugar, 1 tablespoon at a time, and continue beating until stiffly peaking.

Stir a spoonful of egg whites into chocolate mixture to lighten it, then fold in remaining whites. Divide mixture evenly among tartlets, filling them almost to the pastry edge. Bake for 10 to 12 minutes until mixture is just set, but still slightly wobbly. Dust lightly with confectioners' sugar and serve immediately.

pear and chocolate
cream tart

Ingredients

SERVES 6 TO 8

9-INCH TART PAN LINED WITH BASIC SWEET PASTRY OR CHOCOLATE PASTRY (SEE P.50)

4 OZ SEMISWEET CHOCOLATE, MELTED

1 CUP HEAVY CREAM

¼ CUP SUGAR

1 EGG

1 EGG YOLK

1 TSP VANILLA OR ALMOND EXTRACT

3 RIPE PEARS

In a saucepan over low heat, melt chocolate, cream, and half the sugar, stirring frequently, until smooth. Remove from heat and cool slightly. Beat in the egg, egg yolk, and vanilla or almond extract and spread evenly in pastry shell, set on a cookie sheet.

Preheat a 375°F oven. Peel the pears, then halve, and core them. Put them on a work surface cut-side down and cut crosswise into thin slices.

Arrange pears spoke fashion in the pastry shell and press gently with the heel of your hand to fan out pear slices toward the center. Tap tart gently on the work surface to eliminate air bubbles.

Bake for 10 minutes. Reduce oven temperature to 350°F. Sprinkle surface of the tart with remaining sugar and bake until custard is set and pears are tender and glazed, about 20 minutes more. Transfer to a wire rack to cool slightly. Serve warm.

chocolate
banoffee tart

Ingredients

SERVES 6 TO 8

9-INCH TART PAN (DEEP)
LINED WITH CHOCOLATE PASTRY,
BAKED BLIND (SEE P.50)

TWO 14-OZ CANS
SWEETENED CONDENSED MILK

6 OZ GOOD QUALITY
SEMISWEET CHOCOLATE,
CHOPPED

$^2/_3$ CUP HEAVY CREAM

1 TBSP LIGHT CORN SYRUP

3 RIPE BANANAS

FOR THE WHITE
CHOCOLATE CREAM

$1^2/_3$ HEAVY CREAM

$5^1/_2$ OZ GOOD QUALITY WHITE
CHOCOLATE, SHREDDED

$^1/_2$ TSP VANILLA EXTRACT

COCOA POWDER, FOR DUSTING

Puncture the cans of milk (to prevent any possible explosion while cooking). Put in a medium saucepan and add water almost to top of cans. Bring to a boil, then reduce heat, and simmer, covered, for about 2 hours. Be sure to top up with water. (Some milk may leak but this does not matter.) Remove cans from the water and cool.

In a saucepan over medium-low heat, combine chocolate, heavy cream, and syrup. Cook until smooth and melted, stirring constantly. Pour into chocolate pastry shell and chill until set, about 1 hour.

Meanwhile, prepare the white chocolate cream. In a small saucepan over medium heat, bring $^1/_2$ cup of the cream to a boil. Remove from heat and stir in the shredded white chocolate, stirring until completely smooth. Stir in the vanilla extract. Strain into a bowl and cool to room temperature.

Scrape condensed milk into a bowl. Whisk the thickened "toffee" until smooth. Immediately spread evenly over chocolate layer in the pastry shell.

Slice bananas thinly and arrange them in overlapping concentric circles over toffee layer in the pastry shell. In a medium bowl, whisk the remaining cream until stiffly peaking. Fold a spoonful into the white chocolate cream to lighten it, then fold in remaining cream. Spoon over banana layer and spread to the edge. Dust top with cocoa powder. Chill until ready to serve.

coffee and raisin pecan pies

Ingredients

SERVES 6

4 TBSP COARSELY GROUND HIGH ROAST COFFEE

$^2/_3$ CUP HOT WATER

GENEROUS 1 CUP SEEDLESS RAISINS

7 TBSP (1 STICK) SALTED BUTTER

SCANT $^1/_2$ CUP CLEAR HONEY

1 TBSP COFFEE EXTRACT

1$^3/_4$ CUPS PECANS

FOR THE PASTRY

2 CUPS ALL-PURPOSE FLOUR

7 TBSP (1 STICK) SALTED BUTTER

COLD WATER, TO MIX

SIFTED CONFECTIONERS' SUGAR, TO DECORATE

Pour hot water onto coffee and let stand for 10 to 15 minutes. Strain into a small bowl, add raisins, and allow to soak for 10 minutes. Preheat a 400°F oven.

Meanwhile, prepare pastry. Blend butter into the flour until the mixture resembles fine bread crumbs, then bind to a firm, manageable dough with cold water. Divide the dough into six pieces and roll them out to line six 4-inch tartlet pans. Chill pastry shells, about 1 hour.

Drain raisins. Beat butter until soft, then add the honey and coffee extract, and beat until well mixed. Roughly chop half the pecans and add to the butter with the raisins, 2 tablespoons of cold coffee, and coffee extract. Don't worry if the mixture appears curdled. Divide the mixture among pastry shells and smooth it down, then decorate with remaining pecans.

Bake for 10 minutes, then reduce oven temperature to 375°F and cook for 15 minutes more. Allow pies to cool slightly, remove from their pans, then sprinkle generously with confectioners' sugar before serving.

apricot cheesecake

Ingredients

SERVES 8 TO 10

2 CUPS DRIED APRICOTS

1¹/₂ CUPS WATER

SCANT 1 CUP LOWFAT CREAM
CHEESE, OR STRAINED COTTAGE
CHEESE

1 CUP THICK PLAIN YOGURT

1 TBSP POWDERED GELATIN

2 EGG WHITES (SEE NOTE P.4)

FINE STRIPS OF ORANGE RIND,
TO DECORATE

FOR THE BASE

3¹/₂ TBSP (¹/₂ STICK)
UNSALTED BUTTER

3¹/₂ TBSP CLEAR HONEY

2 CUPS NATURAL GRANOLA

Soak apricots in the water for 4 hours. For the base, melt butter in a
pan, then stir in the honey and granola; mix well. Press mixture into the
base of a deep, 8-inch springform pan using the back of a metal spoon.
Chill until required, about 1 hour.

Reserve ¹/₃ cup of liquid from the apricots. Purée the fruit with remaining
juice in a blender until smooth—add a little water if necessary. Turn into
a bowl and beat in the cheese and yogurt. Heat reserved apricot juice
until almost at a boil, then remove from heat and sprinkle gelatin over.
Stir, then leave to stand for 2 minutes, until completely dissolved.
Stir 1 heaping tablespoon of apricot mixture into the gelatin—this helps
to incorporate it evenly—then fold gelatin into apricot mixture. Whisk egg
whites until stiff, then fold them into the apricots.

Pour mixture over the granola base and smooth top. Chill for 3 hours until
set. Remove cheesecake from pan and decorate with orange rind.

blueberry cheesecake

Ingredients

SERVES 6

FOR THE BASE

1 CUP NATURAL GRANOLA

1 CUP DRIED FIGS

FOR THE FILLING

1 TSP POWDERED GELATIN

1/2 CUP SKIM EVAPORATED MILK

1 EGG (SEE NOTE, P.4)

6 TBSP SUPERFINE SUGAR

2 CUPS LOWFAT COTTAGE CHEESE

1/2 CUP BLUEBERRIES

FOR THE TOPPING

2 CUPS BLUEBERRIES

2 NECTARINES, PITTED AND SLICED

1 TBSP CLEAR HONEY

Place granola and dried figs in a food processor and blend together for 30 seconds. Press into a base-lined, 8-inch springform pan and chill while preparing the filling.

Sprinkle gelatin onto 4 tablespoons of cold water. Stir until dissolved and heat to boiling point. Boil for about 2 minutes. Cool. Place milk, egg, sugar, and cheese in a food processor and blend until smooth. Stir in the blueberries. Place in a mixing bowl and gradually stir in the dissolved gelatin. Pour mixture into the base and chill for 2 hours until set.

Remove cheesecake from the pan and arrange fruit for the topping in alternate rings on top. Drizzle honey over the fruit and serve.

orange cardamom tart

Ingredients

SERVES 6 TO 8

9-INCH TART PAN LINED
WITH BASIC SWEET PASTRY,
PARTIALLY BAKED BLIND (SEE P.50)

5 TBSP FINE-CUT ORANGE
MARMALADE

1½ CUPS SUGAR

1¼ CUPS FRESHLY SQUEEZED
ORANGE JUICE, STRAINED

2 LARGE NAVEL ORANGES,
SLICED THINLY

8 TBSP (1 STICK) UNSALTED
BUTTER, SOFTENED

2 EGGS

2 EGG YOLKS

²/3 CUP HEAVY CREAM

SEEDS FROM 4 OR 5 CARDAMOM
PODS, LIGHTLY CRUSHED

SHREDDED RIND OF 3 ORANGES

⅓ CUP GOLDEN RAISINS, PLUMPED

In a small saucepan over low heat, heat 3 tablespoons of marmalade until melted. Use to brush bottom of the pastry shell with an even layer. Set on a cookie sheet for easier handling.

Combine half the sugar and 1 cup of the orange juice. Bring to a boil and cook until thick and syrupy, about 10 minutes. Add orange slices to the syrup and simmer gently until completely glazed, about 10 minutes. Carefully transfer to a wire rack set over a cookie sheet to catch any drips. Reserve syrup to use later.

Preheat a 375°F oven. With an electric mixer, beat butter, eggs, egg yolks and remaining sugar until lightened, about 2 minutes. Gradually beat in the cream, cardamom seeds, and remaining marmalade. Stir in the orange rind, remaining juice, and golden raisins.

Pour mixture into the sweet pastry shell. Bake until filling is just set, about 35 minutes. Transfer to a wire rack to cool slightly. Arrange orange slices in overlapping concentric circles on top of the tart. Bring reserved syrup to a boil and brush over orange slices to glaze. Serve at room temperature.

lemon tart

Ingredients

SERVES 6 TO 8

**9-INCH TART PAN LINED
WITH BASIC SWEET PASTRY,
PARTIALLY BAKED BLIND**
(SEE P.50)

GRATED RIND OF 2-3 LEMONS

**5 FL OZ FRESHLY
SQUEEZED LEMON JUICE**

1/2 CUP SUGAR

1/2 CUP HEAVY CREAM

3 EGGS

3 EGG YOLKS

**CONFECTIONERS'
SUGAR FOR DUSTING**

Preheat oven to 375°F. With an electric mixer on low speed, beat together lemon rind, juice, and sugar. Slowly beat in the cream until blended, then beat in eggs and yolks, one at a time.

Set tart case on a cookie sheet for easier handling and carefully pour in the filling. (If you prefer a completely smooth filling, strain into tart case, removing rind.)

Bake until filling is just set, but not colored, about 20 minutes. If tart begins to color, cover with foil. Transfer to a wire rack to cool completely. Dust lightly with confectioners' sugar before serving.

basic sweet pastry

Ingredients

FOR A 9 TO 10 INCH TART PAN

1½ CUPS ALL-PURPOSE FLOUR

½ TSP SALT

3-4 TBSP CONFECTIONERS' SUGAR

8 TBSP (1 STICK) COLD UNSALTED BUTTER, CUT INTO SMALL PIECES

2 EGG YOLKS BEATEN WITH 2 TBSP ICED WATER AND ½ TSP VANILLA EXTRACT (OPTIONAL)

Put flour, salt and sugar in bowl of a food processor, fitted with a metal blade. Process for 5 to 7 seconds. Add butter to flour mixture and process for 10 to 15 seconds or until the mixture resembles coarse crumbs. With the machine running, add yolk-water mixture and process just until pastry begins to hold together.

Test pastry by pinching a piece between your fingers; if it is still crumbly add a little more water and pulse once or twice. Do not allow pastry to form into a ball at this stage because the baked crust will toughen. Turn out the pastry on to a sheet of plastic wrap.

Using the plastic wrap as a guide, knead gently until pastry is just blended. Flatten into a disc and cover with plastic wrap. Refrigerate for 1 hour. To partially blind bake, set oven to 400°F and bake for 15 to 20 minutes, weighting pastry with a layer of foil and dried beans.

chocolate pastry

Ingredients

FOR A 9 TO 10-INCH TART PAN

8 TBSP (1 STICK) UNSALTED BUTTER, SOFTENED

⅓ CUP SUPERFINE SUGAR

½ TSP SALT

2 TSP VANILLA EXTRACT

½ CUP COCOA POWDER

1½ CUPS ALL-PURPOSE FLOUR

Put butter, sugar, salt, and vanilla into bowl of a food processor fitted with a metal blade and process for 25 to 30 seconds. Add cocoa and process, about 1 minute. Add flour all at once and process for 10 to 15 seconds until it is well blended. Turn pastry out on to a sheet of plastic wrap and shape into a flat circle. Wrap and refrigerate, 1 hour.

Soften pastry for 10 to 15 minutes at room temperature. Unwrap and sandwich between two large pieces of plastic wrap. Carefully roll out to 11-inch round, about ¼ inch thick. Peel off top sheet and invert pastry into a greased tart tin. Gently ease pastry on to the bottom and sides of the tin, then remove the bottom layer of wrap. Press pastry into tin, then cut off any excess. Prick base of pastry with a fork and chill for 1 hour.

Preheat oven to 400°F. Blind bake for 10 minutes weighting pastry with a layer of foil and dried beans. Then remove foil and beans and bake for 5 more minutes until just set. Transfer to a wire rack to cool.

uxuriate in i

cakes & bakes

apple cake

Ingredients

SERVES 12

$^1/_2$ CUP PLUS
2 TBSP APPLE SAUCE

$^1/_2$ CUP PLUS
2 TBSP BROWN SUGAR

3 TBSP SKIM MILK

$1^1/_2$ CUPS ALL-PURPOSE FLOUR

$^1/_3$ CUP ALL BRAN CEREAL

2 TSP BAKING POWDER

1 TSP GROUND CINNAMON

2 TBSP CLEAR HONEY

5 OZ DESSERT APPLES,
PEELED AND CHOPPED

2 EGG WHITES

DESSERT APPLE SLICES
AND 1 TBSP CLEAR HONEY,
TO DECORATE

Preheat a 150°F oven. Grease and base line a deep 8-inch round cake pan.

Place apple sauce in a mixing bowl with the sugar and milk. Sift flour into the bowl and add All Bran, baking powder, cinnamon, honey, and apples. Whisk egg whites until peaking and fold into the mixture. Spoon mixture into cake pan and level the surface.

Bake for $1^1/_4$ to $1^1/_2$ hours or until cooked through. Cool in pan for 10 minutes, then turn onto a wire rack, and cool completely. To serve, arrange apple slices on top and drizzle with honey.

pear upside-down cake

Ingredients

SERVES 8

2 TBSP CLEAR HONEY

2 TBSP GRANULATED
BROWN SUGAR

2 LARGE PEARS, PEELED,
CORED, AND SLICED

4 TBSP ($^1/_2$ STICK) BUTTER

$^1/_4$ CUP SUPERFINE SUGAR

3 EGG WHITES

1 CUP SELF-RISING FLOUR

2 TSP GROUND ALLSPICE

WALNUT HALVES, TO DECORATE

Preheat a 350°F oven. Heat honey and brown sugar in a pan until melted. Pour into a base-lined, 8-inch round cake pan. Arrange pears around the base of the pan.

Cream butter and sugar together until light and fluffy. Whisk egg whites until peaking and fold into the mixture with the flour and allspice. Spoon on top of the pears and level the surface.

Bake for 50 minutes or until risen and golden. Let stand for 5 minutes, then turn out onto a serving plate. Remove the lining paper and decorate with walnuts before serving.

mocha gateau aux noix

Ingredients

SERVES 8 TO 10

GENEROUS 1 CUP FLOUR

PINCH OF SALT

3 TBSP (1/3 STICK)
UNSALTED BUTTER

3 EGGS

1/2 CUP SUPERFINE SUGAR

2 TBSP STRONG COLD COFFEE

FOR THE FROSTING

1/2 LB (2 STICKS) UNSALTED
BUTTER, SOFTENED

4 TBSP STRONG COLD COFFEE

1 3/4 CUPS CONFECTIONERS'
SUGAR, SIFTED

SCANT 1 CUP WALNUT HALVES

Preheat a 350°F oven and line an 8-inch round cake pan with baking
parchment. Sift flour and salt together. Melt butter and let cool. Whisk the
eggs and sugar with an electric beater until pale and very thick.

Sift the flour again, then add it to the mixture one third at a time, folding
in lightly with a wire whisk. Add cooled butter and coffee with the last lot
of flour. Turn mixture into prepared pan and bake for 30 to 40 minutes,
until lightly golden. The cake will shrink slightly from the sides when
ready, and should spring back when lightly touched. Remove cake from
the pan, and let cool on a wire rack.

For the frosting, beat the butter until creamy, then add the coffee.
Gradually beat in the confectioners' sugar. If you prefer a very buttery,
French-style frosting, use only about two thirds of the sugar.

Slice the cake horizontally in half and spread bottom half with frosting.
Sandwich the layers together, then frost the top, reserving enough to
pipe around the edge in swirls. Decorate with walnut halves and serve.

chocolate coconut cake

Ingredients

SERVES 6 TO 8

4 EGG YOLKS

3 TBSP (1/3 STICK) UNSALTED BUTTER

1 1/2 CUPS SUGAR

1/2 CUP MILK

1 TSP VANILLA EXTRACT

2 CUPS FLOUR, SIFTED

1 CUP COCOA POWDER, SIFTED

1 1/2 TBSP BAKING POWDER

4 EGG WHITES, BEATEN UNTIL STIFFLY PEAKING

FOR THE FILLING

7-OZ CAN SWEETENED CONDENSED MILK

3/4 CUP MILK

5 CUPS SHREDDED COCONUT

FOR THE TOPPING

7-OZ CAN SWEETENED CONDENSED MILK

1/2 CUP MILK

3 TBSP COCOA POWDER

1/2 TBSP BUTTER

Preheat a 375°F oven. Beat together egg yolks, butter, and sugar. Add milk and vanilla. Then add flour and cocoa, and beat for 5 minutes more. Add baking powder and fold in egg whites.

Pour cake mixture into a 12-inch cake pan and bake in oven for 25 to 30 minutes, until firm to touch.

For the filling, put all ingredients into a saucepan and cook over low heat for 3 minutes, stirring continuously, until mixture starts to come away from edges of pan. Use same method for the cake topping.

When the cake is baked, remove from the pan and let cool on a wire rack. When cool, cut cake in half horizontally. Spread filling over the bottom half, replace top half, and then spread the topping over. Decorate with extra shredded coconut scattered on top, if you wish.

hazelnut-plum coffee cake

Ingredients

SERVES 8

1/2 CUP WHOLE HAZELNUTS, LIGHTLY TOASTED

1/2 CUP FIRMLY PACKED, LIGHT BROWN SUGAR

1/3 CUP FLOUR

1/2 TSP FRESHLY GRATED NUTMEG

3 EGG WHITES

1/8 TSP CREAM OF TARTAR

2 TBSP SUPERFINE SUGAR

1 TSP VANILLA EXTRACT

3 TBSP (1/3 STICK) UNSALTED BUTTER, MELTED AND COOLED

2-3 RIPE PLUMS, SLICED THINLY

CONFECTIONERS' SUGAR, FOR DUSTING

SOUR CREAM, TO DECORATE

Preheat a 425°F oven. Generously butter and flour an 8-inch springform pan. Process the hazelnuts, brown sugar, flour, and nutmeg in a food processor until finely ground.

With an electric mixer, beat egg whites until frothy. Add cream of tartar and beat until just stiff. Sprinkle over 1 tablespoon of superfine sugar and beat for 30 seconds longer until whites are stiff and glossy.

Sprinkle nut mixture over egg whites and fold in gently. Stir vanilla into the melted butter, and slowly drizzle the butter down the side of the bowl; fold in gently (don't worry if batter deflates). Spoon into cake pan and smooth over the top.

Arrange plum slices in concentric circles over batter, and sprinkle with remaining superfine sugar. Bake until golden, and cake begins to shrink away from side of pan, 20 to 25 minutes. Remove to a wire rack to cool. Run a sharp knife between cake and side of pan; unclip and remove the side. Dust top with confectioners' sugar, and serve warm, with a spoonful of sour cream, if desired.

passionfruit-glazed pound cake

Ingredients

SERVES 8 TO 10

1¹/₂ CUPS FLOUR

³/₄ TSP BAKING POWDER

12 TBSP (1¹/₂ STICKS) UNSALTED BUTTER, SOFTENED

1 CUP SUGAR

SHREDDED RIND OF 1 ORANGE

1 TSP VANILLA EXTRACT

3 EGGS, LIGHTLY BEATEN

FOR THE PASSIONFRUIT GLAZE

8-10 RIPE PASSIONFRUIT

ABOUT ¹/₃ CUP SUGAR

4 SEEDLESS ORANGES, PEELED AND SEGMENTED

CONFECTIONERS' SUGAR, FOR DUSTING (OPTIONAL)

Preheat a 350°F oven. Grease 9 x 5-inch loaf pan and line with non-stick baking parchment. Grease the paper and dust pan lightly with flour. Sift flour and baking powder into a bowl.

Beat butter until light and creamy, for 1 to 2 minutes with an electric mixer. Gradually beat in sugar until light and fluffy, then beat in the orange rind and vanilla extract. Beat in eggs on low speed until well blended. Fold flour mixture into the egg mixture until just blended. Scrape into pan, smoothing top evenly. Bake until risen and golden, and a metal skewer inserted into the center comes out clean, about 1 hour. Leave in pan and place on a wire rack to cool.

To prepare glaze, cut six of the passionfruit crosswise in half, and scoop pulp into a nylon strainer placed over a bowl. Press through with a wooden spoon. Stir in about ¹/₃ cup sugar; the amount required will depend on the sweetness of the passionfruit. Stir until sugar is dissolved. Using a long metal skewer, pierce 30 holes from top to bottom all over the cake. Slowly spoon over the glaze and let stand for about 20 minutes. Carefully unmold onto rack, top-side up. Dust generously with confectioners' sugar before serving.

Meanwhile, cut the remaining passionfruit crosswise in half, and then scoop the pulp into a bowl; sweeten to taste with 2 to 3 tablespoons of sugar. Serve cake with a few orange segments drizzled with passionfruit glaze.

gingerbread

Ingredients

SERVES 9

2 CUPS FLOUR

2 TSP BAKING POWDER

1¹/₂ TSP BAKING SODA

¹/₂ TSP SALT

1 TSP GROUND CINNAMON

1 TSP GROUND GINGER

¹/₂ TSP FRESHLY GRATED
NUTMEG

¹/₄ TSP GROUND CLOVES

¹/₈ TSP FRESHLY GROUND
BLACK PEPPER

8 TBSP (1 STICK) BUTTER

¹/₄ CUP SUGAR

¹/₂ CUP MOLASSES
(PREFERABLY DARK)

¹/₄ CUP CLEAR HONEY

1 EGG, LIGHTLY BEATEN

1 TSP VANILLA EXTRACT

¹/₂ CUP BUTTERMILK

WHIPPED HEAVY CREAM WITH
MAPLE SYRUP, TO SERVE

Preheat a 350°F oven. Grease and flour a 9-inch square cake pan. Sift flour, baking powder, baking soda, salt, cinnamon, ginger, nutmeg, cloves, and pepper into a bowl.

In a large bowl with an electric mixer, beat butter and sugar until light and fluffy, for 1 or 2 minutes. On low speed, beat in molasses and honey until well blended, scraping down side of bowl once. Then beat in egg and vanilla extract.

Lightly stir in the flour mixture and buttermilk alternately in batches until well blended. Scrape batter into pan and bake until risen and golden, and a metal skewer comes out with just a crumb or two attached, about 35 to 40 minutes.

Remove to a wire rack to cool, about 10 minutes, then unmold onto rack top-side up. Serve warm with a spoonful of thick, whipped heavy cream, flavored with maple syrup.

english scones

Ingredients

MAKES ABOUT 15 SCONES

3 CUPS FLOUR

1¹/2 TSP BAKING SODA

¹/2 TSP SALT

3 TBSP SUGAR

6 TBSP (³/4 STICK) UNSALTED BUTTER, CUT INTO PIECES

¹/3 CUP SEEDLESS CURRANTS OR RAISINS

1 EGG, LIGHTLY BEATEN

1¹/4 CUPS BUTTERMILK

2 TBSP MILK

CLOTTED CREAM OR LIGHTLY WHIPPED HEAVY CREAM, TO SERVE

STRAWBERRY PRESERVE, TO SERVE

Preheat a 425°F oven. Lightly flour a large cookie sheet. Sift flour, baking soda, and salt into a large bowl, then stir in sugar until well blended.

Scatter butter pieces over flour mixture, and rub in the butter until mixture resembles bread crumbs. Blend in the currants or raisins, and make a well in the center.

Beat egg with ³/4 cup of buttermilk, and pour into well. Stir flour mixture into the liquid with a fork until it is combined. Form the dough into a rough ball, and place on a lightly floured surface. Knead lightly, eight to ten times, until blended.

Roll the dough into a ³/4-inch thick round. Use a floured, 2¹/2-inch round cutter to cut out as many rounds as possible. Transfer to the cookie sheet, arranging them about 1 inch apart.

Brush tops of scones with a little milk, and bake until risen and golden, about 15 minutes. Remove to a wire rack to cool slightly. Serve warm with fresh, whipped heavy cream and strawberry preserve.

lemon-cream scones with fresh lemon curd

Ingredients

MAKES 9 SCONES

2 CUPS FLOUR

1 TBSP BAKING POWDER

1/2 TSP SALT

1/3 CUP SUGAR

3/4 CUP (ABOUT 4 OZ) CHOPPED, READY-TO-EAT DRIED APRICOTS

SHREDDED RIND OF 1 LARGE LEMON

1 1/4 CUPS HEAVY CREAM

CONFECTIONERS' SUGAR, FOR DUSTING

WHIPPED HEAVY CREAM, TO SERVE (OPTIONAL)

Preheat a 425°F oven. Lightly flour a large cookie sheet. Sift flour, baking powder, and salt into a large bowl. Stir in the sugar, dried apricots, and lemon rind, and make a well in the center.

Add 1 1/4 cups of cream, and stir lightly until a soft dough forms, adding more cream if necessary. Form into a rough ball and place on a lightly floured surface. Knead five to six times until just combined. Roll or pat dough into a 3/4-inch thick square about 8 x 8 inches. Cut into nine squares. Alternatively, use a floured 2 1/2 to 3-inch cutter to cut into rounds (see English Scones, page 59).

Arrange the squares or rounds on the cookie sheet, about 1 inch apart. Bake until risen and golden, 10 to 14 minutes. Place cookie sheet on a wire rack for about 2 minutes, then transfer scones to wire rack to cool to room temperature. Dust lightly with confectioners' sugar, and serve warm with lemon curd and a spoonful of whipped heavy cream.

fresh lemon curd

MAKES ABOUT 2 CUPS

SHREDDED RIND AND JUICE OF 1 LARGE LEMON

12 TBSP (1 1/2 STICKS) UNSALTED BUTTER, CUT INTO PIECES

1 CUP SUGAR

1/4 TSP SALT

3 EGGS, LIGHTLY BEATEN

Put lemon rind, lemon juice, butter, sugar, and salt in a heatproof bowl. Place over a saucepan of just-simmering water; and stir gently until the butter melts.

Whisk eggs into butter mixture, then cook over low heat until mixture thickens, about 15 minutes. Do not allow to boil, or the mixture will curdle. Pour or strain into a bowl, and press a piece of plastic wrap directly against the surface to prevent a skin from forming. Chill before serving.

cranberry-orange scones with cranberry-raspberry butter

Ingredients

MAKES ABOUT 10 SCONES

3 CUPS FLOUR

1 TBSP BAKING POWDER

1/2 TSP SALT

2 TBSP SUGAR, PLUS EXTRA FOR SPRINKLING

SHREDDED RIND OF 1 ORANGE

4 TBSP (1/2 STICK) UNSALTED BUTTER, CUT INTO PIECES

3/4 CUP DRIED CRANBERRIES

2 EGGS

1/2-2/3 CUP HEAVY CREAM, PLUS EXTRA FOR GLAZING

1/2 TSP VANILLA EXTRACT

2 TBSP MILK

2 TBSP FIRMLY PACKED, LIGHT BROWN SUGAR

Preheat a 425°F oven. Lightly flour a large cookie sheet. Sift flour, baking powder, and salt into a large bowl; stir in sugar and orange rind. Scatter butter pieces over flour mixture, and blend in the butter using a pastry blender or your fingertips, until mixture resembles medium bread crumbs. Stir in dried cranberries, and make a well in the center.

In a small bowl, beat egg and 1/2 cup of the cream until well blended; beat in vanilla extract and pour into the liquid just until it begins to combine; do not overmix. Form dough into a rough ball and place on a lightly floured surface. Knead six to eight times until blended. Pat dough into a 3/4-inch thick round and cut out as many rounds as possible using a 2 1/2-inch floured cutter. Transfer to the cookie sheet, arranging them 1 inch apart to allow space when cooking.

Brush top of scones with a little more cream or milk, and sprinkle with sugar. Bake until risen and golden, about 12 minutes. Transfer scones onto wire rack to cool. Serve with Cranberry-Raspberry Butter.

cranberry-raspberry butter

MAKES ABOUT 1 1/2 CUPS

12 TBSP (1 1/2 STICKS) UNSALTED BUTTER, SOFTENED

1 TBSP CRANBERRY SAUCE

1 TBSP RASPBERRY PRESERVE

1 TBSP ORANGE JUICE

1/2 TSP GROUND CINNAMON

Beat butter until smooth and creamy in a small bowl. Beat in cranberry sauce, preserve, orange juice, and ground cinnamon until well blended. Scrape into a bowl and chill, covered, until ready to serve.

double chocolate-chip muffins

Ingredients

MAKES 10 MUFFINS

1³/4 CUPS FLOUR

¹/4 CUP COCOA POWDER

1 TBSP BAKING POWDER

¹/2 TSP SALT

¹/2 CUP SUGAR

¹/2 CUP SEMISWEET CHOCOLATE CHIPS

¹/4 CUP WHITE CHOCOLATE CHIPS

2 EGGS

¹/2 CUP SUNFLOWER OR VEGETABLE OIL

1 CUP MILK

1 TSP VANILLA EXTRACT

Preheat a 400°F oven. Line ten muffin-pan cups with foil or double-paper liners. Half fill any remaining empty cups in muffin pan with water to prevent them from scorching. Sift flour, cocoa powder, baking powder, and salt into a large bowl. Gradually stir in sugar and chocolate chips, and make a well in the center.

In another bowl, beat eggs with oil until foamy. Gradually beat in milk and vanilla extract. Pour this mixture into well and stir until just combined. Do not overmix; the batter should be slightly lumpy and textured.

Spoon batter into prepared cups, filling each about three-quarters full. Bake until risen, golden, and springy when pressed with your fingertip, about 20 minutes. Remove pan to a wire rack to cool for about 2 minutes, then remove muffins to the wire rack to cool. Serve just warm or at room temperature.

very blue
blueberry muffins

Ingredients

MAKES 12 MUFFINS

2 CUPS FLOUR

2$^1/_2$ TSP BAKING POWDER

$^1/_2$ TSP SALT

$^1/_4$ TSP FRESHLY GRATED NUTMEG

$^3/_4$ CUP SUGAR

2 EGGS

$^3/_4$ CUP MILK

8 TBSP (1 STICK) BUTTER, MELTED AND COOLED

SHREDDED RIND OF HALF AN ORANGE

1 TSP VANILLA EXTRACT

$^1/_2$ CUP FRESH BLUEBERRIES, MASHED

2 CUPS FRESH BLUEBERRIES

$^1/_4$ CUP GRANULATED SUGAR, MIXED WITH $^1/_4$ TSP FRESHLY GRATED NUTMEG, FOR SPRINKLING

Preheat a 375°F oven. Lightly grease a 12-cup muffin pan or line each cup with a paper liner. Sift flour, baking powder, salt, and nutmeg into a large bowl; stir in sugar, and make a well in the center.

In another bowl, beat eggs, milk, melted butter or margarine, orange rind, and vanilla extract; then stir in the mashed blueberries. Pour this mixture into well and lightly stir, until blended in. Do not overmix. Lightly fold in fresh blueberries.

Spoon batter into prepared muffin cups, filling each three-quarters full. Sprinkle each with the sugar-nutmeg mixture, and bake until risen and golden (a metal skewer inserted in the center should come out with a few crumbs attached), 25 to 30 minutes. Remove pan to a wire rack to cool for about 2 minutes, then remove muffins to the wire rack to cool. Serve just warm or at room temperature.

peanut and white chocolate cookies

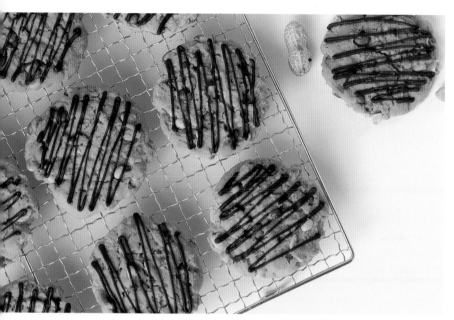

Ingredients

MAKES ABOUT 18 COOKIES

1 CUP FRESHLY SHELLED PEANUTS

1 CUP FLOUR

1/2 TSP BAKING SODA

1/4 TSP SALT

1/2 CUP CHUNKY PEANUT BUTTER

8 TBSP (1 STICK) UNSALTED
BUTTER, SOFTENED

1/2 CUP FIRMLY PACKED LIGHT
BROWN SUGAR

2 TBSP SUGAR

1 EGG

1 TSP VANILLA EXTRACT

6 OZ GOOD QUALITY WHITE
CHOCOLATE, CHOPPED ROUGHLY

2 OZ SEMISWEET
CHOCOLATE, MELTED

In a skillet over medium-low heat, toast the peanuts until golden and fragrant, about 5 minutes, stirring frequently. Turn onto a plate and allow to cool, about 10 to 15 minutes.

Preheat a 375°F oven. Into a medium bowl, sift together flour, baking soda, and salt. In a large bowl with an electric mixer, beat peanut butter, butter, and sugars together until light and fluffy, about 2 to 3 minutes. Add the egg and continue beating 2 minutes more. Beat in vanilla extract. Stir in flour mixture until well blended; then stir in chopped white chocolate and toasted peanuts.

Drop heaping tablespoonfuls at least 2 inches apart on two large cookie sheets, and flatten slightly with the back of a moistened spoon. Bake until golden brown, about 12 to 15 minutes; do not overbake or cookies will be dry. Remove cookie sheets to wire racks to cool for 3 to 5 minutes. Then, using a spatula, remove cookies to wire racks to cool completely.

Spoon melted semisweet chocolate into a wax paper cone and snip off the tip. Drizzle the chocolate over cookies in a zig-zag pattern. Allow to set, then store cookies in an airtight container.

chocolate-orange hearts

Ingredients

MAKES ABOUT 30 COOKIES

2 OZ SEMISWEET CHOCOLATE, CHOPPED

2^1/$_4$ CUPS FLOUR

1^1/$_2$ TSP BAKING POWDER

^{1}/$_4$ TSP SALT

12 TBSP (1^1/$_2$ STICKS) UNSALTED BUTTER, SOFTENED

^{3}/$_4$ CUP SUGAR

1 EGG

1 TSP VANILLA EXTRACT

SHREDDED RIND OF 1 ORANGE

1 TBSP ORANGE JUICE

SUPERFINE SUGAR, FOR SPRINKLING

In a small heatproof bowl set over a saucepan of simmering water, melt chocolate until smooth. Set aside to cool.

Into a medium bowl, sift together flour, baking powder, and salt. In a large bowl with electric mixer, beat the butter and sugar until light and creamy, 1 to 2 minutes. Beat in egg, vanilla extract, orange rind, and juice until well blended. On low speed, beat in flour until a soft dough forms. Remove half the dough, wrap tightly in plastic wrap, and chill thoroughly until firm, about 2 hours.

With mixer on low speed, beat the melted, cooled chocolate into the remaining dough. Wrap in plastic wrap and chill until firm.

Grease and flour two large cookie sheets. On a lightly floured surface, roll out half the orange-flavor dough, ^{1}/$_8$ inch thick (keep the remaining dough chilled). With a floured, 3^1/$_4$-inch heart-shaped cutter, cut out as many hearts as possible. Place ^{1}/$_2$ inch apart on cookie sheets and chill. Repeat with chocolate dough, cutting an equal number of chocolate hearts, and place on another cookie sheet. Chill until firm, about 20 minutes.

Preheat a 350°F oven. With a 2^1/$_8$-inch floured heart-shaped cutter, carefully cut another heart from center of each 3^1/$_4$-inch heart. Place smaller orange hearts in larger chocolate hearts and smaller chocolate hearts in larger orange hearts. With a 1-inch heart-shaped cutter, cut small hearts from center of each cookie, and place small orange hearts into medium chocolate hearts, and small chocolate hearts into medium orange hearts, to achieve desired pattern.

Sprinkle cookies with a little superfine sugar. Bake until golden, about 10 minutes. Remove cookies to wire racks to cool.

triple chocolate
chunk cookies

Ingredients

MAKES ABOUT 18 COOKIES

9 OZ SEMISWEET CHOCOLATE, CHOPPED

12 TBSP (1¹/2 STICKS) UNSALTED BUTTER, CUT INTO PIECES

3 EGGS

³/4 CUP SUGAR

¹/3 CUP LIGHT BROWN SUGAR

2 TSP VANILLA EXTRACT

¹/2 CUP FLOUR

6 TBSP COCOA POWDER, SIFTED

1¹/2 TSP BAKING POWDER

¹/4 TSP SALT

1¹/2 CUPS SEMISWEET CHOCOLATE CHIPS

6 OZ GOOD QUALITY MILK CHOCOLATE, CHOPPED INTO ¹/4-INCH PIECES

6 OZ GOOD QUALITY WHITE CHOCOLATE, CHOPPED INTO ¹/4-INCH PIECES

1¹/2 CUPS PECANS OR WALNUTS, TOASTED AND CHOPPED

Preheat a 325°F oven. Lightly grease two cookie sheets. In a saucepan over low heat, melt the semisweet chocolate and butter, stirring frequently until smooth. Remove from heat to cool slightly.

In a large bowl, with an electric mixer, beat eggs and sugars until light and fluffy, about 2 to 3 minutes. On low speed, gradually beat in melted chocolate and vanilla extract until well blended. Into a small bowl, sift together flour, cocoa powder, baking powder, and salt; then gently stir into chocolate mixture. Stir in the unmelted chocolate chips, pieces, and nuts.

Drop heaping tablespoonfuls, at least 4 inches apart, onto the cookie sheets. Moisten the bottom of a drinking glass and flatten each dough round slightly, to make each cookie about 3 inches round; you will only fit four to six cookies on each cookie sheet, so will need to work in batches. Bake for 10 minutes until tops are cracked and shiny.

Remove the cookie sheets to wire racks to cool slightly. Then, using a metal spatula, carefully remove the cookies to wire racks to cool. Repeat this process with the remaining cookie dough.

chocolate-dipped palmiers

Ingredients

MAKES ABOUT **40** COOKIES

$1/2$ CUP HAZELNUTS, CHOPPED FINELY

2 TBSP SUGAR

$1/2$ TSP GROUND CINNAMON

SUGAR, FOR ROLLING

8 OZ FRESH OR FROZEN PUFF PASTRY, DEFROSTED

1 EGG, LIGHTLY BEATEN

8 OZ SEMISWEET CHOCOLATE

Lightly grease two large cookie sheets. In a small bowl, combine hazelnuts, sugar, and cinnamon. Set aside.

Cut pastry into quarters. Generously sprinkle work surface with sugar and roll out one quarter of pastry to a thin rectangle. Lightly brush pastry with beaten egg, and sprinkle evenly with nut-spice mixture. Fold the long edges of the pastry inward to meet, edge to edge, in the center. Brush surface with a little more beaten egg and sprinkle with more nut-spice mixture. Then fold outside edges inward to meet, edge to edge, in the center to make four even layers.

Preheat a 425°F oven. Using a sharp knife, cut the pastry crosswise into 1-inch strips, and place $1/2$ inch apart on cookie sheets. Open from center fold to form a "V" shape. Chill for 15 minutes.

Bake until golden, about 10 minutes, turning over after 5 minutes. Remove the cookie sheets to wire racks to cool slightly. Then gently remove palmiers to wire racks to cool completely.

In a small heatproof bowl set over a saucepan of just-simmering water, melt chocolate until smooth, stirring frequently. Line cookie sheets with wax paper or foil. Dip each palmier halfway into the chocolate and place on lined cookie sheets. Allow to set before serving.

rich cardamom cookies

Ingredients

**MAKES ABOUT 2 DOZEN
COOKIES**

2 CUPS CAKE FLOUR

4 TSP GROUND CARDAMOM

1/4 TSP SALT

**12 TBSP (1 1/2 STICKS)
UNSALTED BUTTER, SOFTENED**

1/2 CUP SUPERFINE SUGAR

**1/2 CUP SLICED
OR FLAKED ALMONDS**

TO DECORATE

**1/3 CUP CONFECTIONERS'
SUGAR**

1 1/2 TSP CARDAMOM

SLICED OR FLAKED ALMONDS

Preheat oven to 375°F. Grease two large cookie sheets. Into a medium bowl, sift together flour, cardamom, and salt.

In a large bowl with electric mixer, beat butter until creamy, about 30 seconds. Gradually add sugar and continue beating until light and fluffy, 1 to 2 minutes. On low speed, gradually beat in flour mixture until well-blended, then stir in almonds.

Into a small bowl, sift together confectioners' sugar and cardamom. Using a tablespoon, scoop out dough and roll into 1 1/2-inch balls. Drop balls one at a time into the sugar-spice mixture, coating well. Place 1 1/2 inches apart on cookie sheets. Dip the bottom of a glass into sugar mixture, and flatten cookies to 1/2-inch thick rounds. Press a few sliced or flaked almonds onto tops of cookies.

Bake cookies until golden brown, about 12 to 14 minutes. Remove cookie sheets to wire racks to cool, 2 to 3 minutes. Then, using a thin metal palette knife, remove cookies to wire racks to cool completely. Store in airtight containers.

rise to i

breads & pastries

rice fritters

Ingredients

MAKES 45 RICE FRITTERS

1 PACKAGE (2¹/₄ TSP) ACTIVE DRY YEAST

¹/₂ CUP SUGAR

¹/₂ CUP WARM WATER, 105–115°F

2 EGGS

1 TBSP VANILLA EXTRACT

³/₄ TSP SALT

³/₄ TSP NUTMEG

³/₄ TSP SHREDDED LEMON RIND

3 CUPS ALL-PURPOSE OR BREAD FLOUR

3 CUPS COOKED, COOLED RICE

OIL FOR FRYING

CONFECTIONERS' SUGAR

Dissolve yeast and 1 teaspoon of sugar in the warm water. Let yeast built up a foamy head, 5 to 10 minutes.

With a fork, lightly beat remaining sugar with the eggs. Add vanilla, salt, and nutmeg. Mix lemon rind with a little of the flour and add it to the egg mixture. Put flour and rice in a large bowl. Stir in the egg mixture. When yeast is ready, stir it into the flour. Stir or knead dough in the bowl for a few minutes, until it is well mixed. It will be sticky, more like batter than dough. Loosely cover bowl and leave it in a warm place to rise, 1 hour.

Punch down the dough. Let it rest 5 minutes. Then cut off walnut-sized pieces and place on a greased cookie sheet. Cover loosely and put in a warm place to rise, 1 hour.

Pour 3 inches of oil into a deep skillet. Heat oil to 365°F. Slide a few rice balls into the hot oil. They will bob back to the surface. Cook until golden on both sides, about 2 minutes each side. Remove fritters from oil, letting them drain for a few moments. Place on several layers of paper towels and sprinkle with confectioners' sugar. Serve warm.

cinnamon raisin
swirl bread

Ingredients

MAKES 1 LOAF

1 PACKAGE (2¼ TSP) ACTIVE
DRY YEAST

4½ TBSP SUGAR

1¼ CUPS WARM MILK, 105–115°F

ABOUT 3 CUPS ALL-PURPOSE
OR BREAD FLOUR

1½ TBSP (¼ STICK) BUTTER

1½ TSP SALT

6 TBSP RAISINS

2 TBSP (¼ STICK) VERY
SOFT BUTTER

6 TBSP BROWN SUGAR

1½ TSP CINNAMON

Dissolve yeast and a pinch of the sugar in warm milk. Let yeast build up a foamy head, 5 to 10 minutes.

Put about 2½ cups flour in a large bowl. Mix in remaining sugar, 1½ tablespoons butter, salt, and raisins. When yeast is ready, stir it into flour. Turn dough out onto a floured surface. Knead with floured hands, adding flour as needed, for about 10 minutes, until you have a smooth dough, neither sticky nor overly stiff. Place dough in a greased bowl and turn so all surfaces are lightly oiled. Loosely cover bowl and leave in a warm place to rise until it has doubled in bulk, about 1½ hours.

Mix brown sugar and cinnamon. Butter a 9½-inch loaf pan. Punch down the dough. Let it rest 5 minutes. Roll it out on a lightly floured surface to form a rectangle about 8 inches wide and about 16 inches long. Spread the butter, then sprinkle brown sugar mixture over surface of dough. Roll into a fat 8-inch-long cylinder. Tucking edge under, put it in the loaf pan. Loosely cover and put in a warm place to rise, 1 hour.

Bake loaf in a preheated 350°F oven until top is golden and a skewer comes out clean, 25 to 30 minutes. Remove the bread from pan and put it on a wire rack. Let it cool at least 30 minutes before serving.

vanocka (czechoslovakian christmas bread)

Ingredients

MAKES 1 LOAF

1 PACKAGE (2¼ TSP) ACTIVE DRY YEAST

¼ CUP SUGAR

⅔ CUP WARM MILK, 105–115°F

1 EGG

4 TBSP (½ STICK) BUTTER, SOFTENED

1 TSP SALT

¼ TSP GROUND GINGER

¼ TSP GROUND NUTMEG

1 TSP SHREDDED LEMON RIND

ABOUT 3 CUPS ALL-PURPOSE OR BREAD FLOUR

¼ CUP SLIVERED BLANCHED ALMONDS

¼ CUP GOLDEN RAISINS

1 TBSP CANDIED ORANGE PEEL

1 EGG YOLK BEATEN WITH 1 TBSP WATER

2 TBSP SLICED ALMONDS

CONFECTIONERS' SUGAR

Dissolve yeast and 1 teaspoon of sugar in warm milk. Let yeast build up a foamy head, 5 to 10 minutes.

With a fork, lightly beat remaining sugar with the egg. Stir in butter, salt, ginger, and nutmeg. Mix lemon rind with a little of the flour and add it. Put about 2½ cups flour in a large bowl. Stir in the egg mixture. When yeast is ready, stir it into the flour. Turn dough out onto a floured surface. Knead with floured hands, adding flour as needed, for about 10 minutes, until you have a smooth dough, neither sticky nor overly stiff. Place dough in a greased bowl and turn it over so all surfaces are lightly oiled. Loosely cover bowl and leave it in a warm place for dough to rise until it has doubled in bulk, about 1½ hours.

Oil a cookie sheet at least 14 inches long. Punch down dough. Knead in the almonds, raisins, and orange rind. Cut dough into four equal parts. Take three parts and roll each to form a rope about 18 inches long. Braid the ropes, pinch ends together, and place on cookie sheet.

Cut remaining piece into four equal parts. Again, take three and roll each between your hands to form a thin rope about 18 inches long. Braid the ropes and center braid on top of the fat braid. Run wetted fingers along underside of thin braid, then lightly press it into the fat braid. Pinch the ends together and press them under ends of fat braid.

Cut remaining piece into two equal parts. Roll each into a skinny rope about 16 inches long. Twist the two ropes together. Center the twist on the thin braid. Wet your fingers and run them lightly on underside of the twist, then lightly press onto the thin braid. Pinch ends together and turn under. Use several toothpicks to skewer braids in place, otherwise the top braids may slip off as dough rises. Cover bread loosely, put in a warm place, and let rise until dough has almost doubled, about 1 hour.

Preheat the oven to 375°F. Lightly brush with egg wash, then sprinkle sliced almonds over top and press a few into sides. Bake until brown and a skewer comes out clean. Sprinkle with confectioners' sugar while warm.

chocolate
poppy-seed braid

Ingredients

SERVES 12 TO 14

1/4 CUP WATER

1/4 CUP SUGAR

1 PACKAGE FAST-RISING DRIED YEAST

1/4 CUP LUKEWARM MILK

1/2 TSP SALT

1 EGG, LIGHTLY BEATEN

4 TBSP (1/2 STICK) BUTTER

3-3 1/2 CUPS FLOUR

1 EGG YOLK, BEATEN WITH
1 TBSP MILK, FOR GLAZING

**FOR THE CHOCOLATE
POPPY-SEED FILLING**

3/4 CUP POPPY SEEDS

1/4 CUP SUGAR

1/4 CUP RAISINS

1/2 TSP GROUND CINNAMON

SHREDDED RIND OF HALF AN ORANGE

1/4 CUP SOUR CREAM

1 TBSP APRICOT PRESERVE

1/2 CUP SEMISWEET
CHOCOLATE CHIPS

In a small saucepan, heat water and 1 tablespoon of sugar until very warm (120°F to 130°F). Pour into bowl of a heavy-duty electric mixer, and sprinkle over the yeast. Let stand until foamy, about 15 minutes.

Fit the mixer with the dough hook and beat in warm milk, remaining sugar, salt, egg, and butter. On low speed, gradually beat in 3 cups of flour until a soft dough forms. If the dough is very sticky, add a little more flour. Beat until the dough becomes elastic. Turn dough onto a lightly floured surface, and knead until smooth, adding a little more flour if necessary. Place dough in a greased bowl, turning to grease the top. Cover with a clean dish towel, and let rise in a warm place (80°F to 85°F) until doubled in size, about 1 1/2 hours.

Meanwhile, prepare filling. Put all ingredients except the chocolate chips in the bowl of a food processor, and process until just well blended, but not completely smooth. Grease a large cookie sheet.

Punch down the dough, turn onto a lightly floured surface, and gently knead. With a rolling pin, roll into a rectangle about 15 x 10 inches. Transfer to cookie sheet, stretching it gently to keep the shape. Spread filling down center third of dough, to within about 2 inches from each end.

Preheat a 375°F oven. With a sharp knife, cut about ten diagonal slashes from both sides of filling to both edges of the dough, cutting about 1/2 inch from the filling. Beginning at one end, fold the end over the bottom edge of the filling, then fold over all the strips from alternate sides, and tuck ends of the strips under braid. Cover with dish towel and leave in a warm place to rise again until almost doubled in size.

Brush the braid with the egg glaze and bake until golden, about 30 minutes. Remove cookie sheet to a wire rack to cool, 30 minutes, before serving. Serve just warm.

apricot-filled danish ring

Ingredients

SERVES 10 TO 12

1/2 CUP WATER

1/4 CUP SUGAR

1 PACKAGE FAST-RISING DRIED YEAST

2 1/2 CUPS FLOUR

1 TSP SALT

1 EGG, LIGHTLY BEATEN

1/2 TSP VANILLA EXTRACT

1/2 TSP ALMOND EXTRACT

8 OZ (2 STICKS) UNSALTED BUTTER

1 EGG YOLK, BEATEN WITH 1 TBSP WATER, FOR GLAZING

SLIVERED ALMONDS, FOR SPRINKLING

FOR THE APRICOT FILLING

1 CUP READY-TO-EAT DRIED APRICOTS

2 TBSP (1/4 STICK) BUTTER, SOFTENED

2 TBSP CLEAR HONEY OR SUGAR

SHREDDED RIND OF 1 LEMON PLUS 1 TBSP LEMON JUICE

1/2 TSP ALMOND EXTRACT

1-2 TBSP APRICOT PRESERVE

FOR THE GLAZE

1/2 CUP CONFECTIONERS' SUGAR

2-3 TBSP LEMON JUICE

In a small saucepan over low heat, heat water and 1 tablespoon sugar until very warm (120°F to 130°F). Pour into a bowl and sprinkle over the yeast. Let stand until foamy, about 15 minutes. Stir flour, remaining sugar, and salt to blend, and make a well in the center.

Whisk egg, vanilla extract, and almond extract into yeast mixture and pour into well. Stir with a wooden spoon until a rough dough forms. Place on a lightly floured surface and knead until smooth and elastic, about 5 minutes. Wrap in plastic wrap and chill in refrigerator for about 10 minutes while preparing butter.

Put butter between two large sheets of plastic wrap and, with a rolling pin, roll into a rectangular shape. Fold butter in half and roll out again. Repeat until butter is smooth and pliable, but still cold. Flatten to form a 6 x 4-inch rectangle.

With a lightly floured rolling pin, roll the dough to a 18 x 8-inch rectangle, keeping center third thicker than the two outer ends. Put butter rectangle on thicker center of dough and fold bottom third of dough over the butter. Fold top third of dough over bottom to enclose the butter. With the rolling pin, firmly press down the "open edges" to seal the dough to create a neat dough "package."

Turn dough "package" so that the short "open edge" faces you and the folded edge is on the left. Gently roll dough to a rectangle about 18 inches long, keeping edges straight; do not press out the butter. Fold the rectangle in thirds, as for enclosing the butter, and press down edges to seal. Press a finger into one corner to clearly mark the first turn. Wrap dough tightly in plastic wrap, and chill for 30 minutes. Repeat the rolling and folding twice more, wrapping, marking, and chilling dough between each turn. After the third turn, wrap and chill dough for at least 2 hours.

Meanwhile prepare filling. Process filling ingredients in food processor until smooth; set aside. Grease a large cookie sheet.

Soften dough at room temperature, 5 to 10 minutes, for easier rolling.

On a floured surface, roll dough to a rectangle of about 28 x 12 inches. Spread apricot filling to within 1 inch of edges. Beginning at one long side, fold or roll the dough loosely, about three times, jelly-roll style. Transfer to cookie sheet and bring the two ends together. Brush one end with a little water, and pinch edges together to seal, forming a ring.

Using floured kitchen scissors, held perpendicular to the ring, make diagonal snips, 1½ inches apart, into the outer edge of the ring, to within 1 inch of the inner edge. Gently pull and twist every other slice of the ring toward the outer edge. Pull and twist the alternating slices toward the center to expose the spiral effect of the filling. Cover and leave in a warm place to rise again until just doubled in size, about 40 minutes.

Preheat a 400°F oven. Brush with egg glaze and sprinkle with slivered almonds. Bake until golden, about 35 minutes. Allow to cool, about 10 minutes, then slide the ring onto wire rack, top-side up, to cool. While ring is still warm, stir confectioners' sugar and lemon juice together until smooth, then drizzle over ring.

index